MW00490486

£6.95

Hoffnung's
THE MAESTRO

Books by
GERARD HOFFNUNG

The Hoffnung Symphony Orchestra
The Hoffnung Music Festival
The Hoffnung Companion to Music
Hoffnung's Musical Chairs
Hoffnung's Acoustics

Hoffnung's

The Maestro

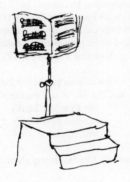

GERARD HOFFNUNG

LONDON 2000

First published 1953
by Dennis Dobson Ltd
2nd impression December 1953
3rd impression March 1954
4th impression December 1954
5th impression October 1955
6th impression December 1956
7th impression October 1957
8th impression December 1958
9th impression September 1960
10th impression November 1963
11th impression January 1968
12th impression December 1972
13th impression October 1975
14th impression December 1977 (Paperback)
15th impression March 1978
16th impression May 1978 (Paperback)
and subsequently re-published by
Souvenir Press from 1983

This edition published 2000
by The Hoffnung Partnership
44 Pilgrims Lane
London NW3 1SN
and reprinted 2004

Copyright © The Hoffnung Partnership 2000

ISBN 1 903643 00 7

Cover and book design
Vera Brice and Leslie Robinson

Printed and bound in Great Britain
by St Edmundsbury Press Ltd
Blenheim Industrial Park, Newmarket Road
Bury St Edmunds, Suffolk IP33 3TZ

To
Annetta, my wife

Acknowledgements

Grateful thanks are due to Sir Simon Rattle for his contribution
to this book, and also to its designers and printers for the
infinite care and consideration they have taken in its production.

Foreword

The Maestro has always been an inspiration to me. It was probably the first hard-back book that I bought with my own pocket money, thinking what an uncanny resemblance *The Maestro* bore to my then music master. At the age of ten, I could hardly have believed that I would be emulating each and every gesture on a daily basis as my profession. Indeed, when I see myself on film, not one of my favourite activities, I sometimes realise that Hoffnung's *Maestro* seems in comparison a model of self control and decorum.

Hoffnung was part of my musical life from the start, something I suspect is true of many musicians and I have been eternally grateful, not only for the sharpness of his observation, but even more for his affection for his fellow musicians. Above all, this was a man of limitless heart and it is this that makes him both immortal and irreplaceable.

So to my old friend, *The Maestro*, *bravo bravissimo* for your achievements over the last fifty years and good luck *con brio* for your journey into this new millennium. I know you will make many new friends along the way and who knows you may have the opportunity for a little amoroso.

Simon Rattle

Alerto

Introduzione

Interruzione

Preciso

Rallentando

Dolce

Affettuoso

Con amore

Con anima

Amoroso

Risoluto

Lusingando

Con delicatezza

Pizzicato

Scherzando

Giocoso

Scherzo

Giojoso

Allegro giocoso

Non troppo

Sotto voce

Piano

Pianissimo

Diminuendo

Molto diminuendo

Tacet

Pomposo

Molto pomposo

Subito piano

A cappella

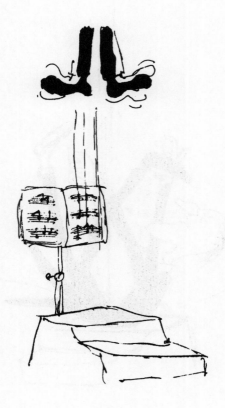

A cappella continuoso

Martellato

Tempo primo

Serioso

Mesto

Doloroso

Molto doloroso

Troppo doloroso

G.P.

Affrettando

Appassionato

Basso

Vigoroso

Con forza

Molto vigoroso

Attacca

Furioso

Rinforzando

Strepitoso

Fortissimo vivacissimo

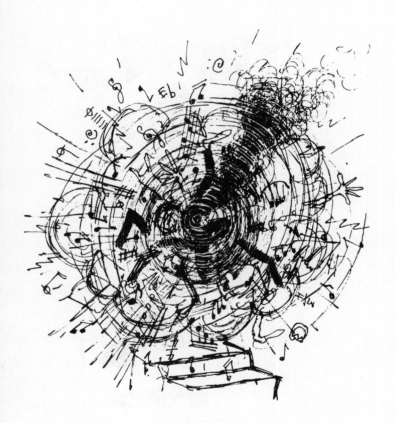

Finale furioso

Bravo bravissimo